MW00628117

A Faith For All Seasons

A Small Group Bible Study Of Life's Changes

Steven Molin

CSS Publishing Company, Inc., Lima, Ohio

A FAITH FOR ALL SEASONS

Scripture quotations marked (GNB) are from the Good News Bible, in Today's English
Version. Copyright © American Bible Society 1966, 1971, 1976. Used by permission.

Scripture quotations marked (NASB) are from the New American Standard Bible © 1960,
1962, 1968, 1972, 1973, 1975, 1977 by The Lockman Foundation. Used by permission.

Scripture quotations marked (NRSV) are from the New Revised Standard Version of the
Bible, copyright 1989 by the Division of Christian Education of the National Council of
the Churches of Christ in the USA. Used by permission.

Doubleday, a division of Random House, Inc., has granted permission to quote from *Tuesdays With Morrie* by Mitch Albom throughout this book.

Fleming H. Revell, a division of Baker Publishing Group, has granted permission to quote
from *Hide or Seek* by James Dobson, in Session Two.

Crossroad Publishing Company has granted permission to quote from *Sabbatical Journey* by Henri Nouwen throughout this book.

Library of Congress Cataloging-in-Publication Data

Molin, Steven, 1950-
A Faith for all seasons : a small group Bible study of life's changes / Steven Molin.
    p. cm.
ISBN 0-7880-2376-4 (perfect bound : alk paper)
1. Bible, O.T. Ecclesiastes III, 1-8—Study and teaching. 2. Bible. O.T. Ecclesiastes III,
1-8b—Criticism, Interpretation, etc. I. Title.

BS1475.52.M65 2005
223'.8'00715—dc22

                        2005015820

For more information about CSS Publishing Company resources, visit our website at
www.csspub.com or email us at custserv@csspub.com or call (800) 241-4056.

Cover design by Jenna Brannon
ISBN 0-7880-2376-4   PRINTED IN U.S.A.

To the members of
Our Savior's Lutheran Church,
Stillwater, Minnesota.
My own, very large
Small Group!

Table Of Contents

Preface

Most high school graduating classes have reunions on the logical anniversaries of their year of graduation: five years, ten years, twenty years, and so on. My high school is different; this summer was the reunion to celebrate the thirty-sixth anniversary of our graduation. I can't explain it!

I was unable to attend the reunion, but I did spend some time paging through that yearbook from 1968. Did we really look like that? Did we actually think those hairstyles and fashions were cool? Apparently so, but what a difference 36 years makes! Today, the class of '68 is wider, shorter, balder, richer, wiser, and better dressed than we were in those days. We have been on a journey of change for 36 years.

The world has changed every bit as much as my classmates and I. Communism is dead, 8-track tapes are no longer available, most moms work outside the home, women can be pastors, my high school closed down, and now I am part of the generation that thinks rock music is too loud!

This is a small group study about change. More precisely, it is a small group study about how the faith of Christian people can endure, survive, and even thrive over the course of change. It was written for the congregation where I serve as pastor in Stillwater, Minnesota, but its focus is much broader than that. It is intended to encourage small groups of people everywhere to refuse to be intimidated by change, because we are held by the one who never changes! May this study draw you closer to God, and closer to one another.

Pastor Steven Molin
Stillwater, Minnesota
September 19, 2004

Session One
Life Is Change

Pastor Mervin Thompson said it best. "There are only two constants in this life: Jesus Christ and change." The implication is obvious, that we go through millions of changes over a lifetime. If you had to list five major changes in your life, you could probably do it off the top of your head (such as moving in the second grade, transitioning from junior high to high school, your parents' divorce, you getting married, being "downsized" at work), and those are just the major changes. What about the minor adjustments you have had to make for sick children, snowstorms, detours in traffic, and a new telephone area code? Change happens! It's a fact of life.

According to Pastor Thompson, the other great constant in life is Jesus Christ. "Jesus Christ is the same yesterday, today, and forever" (Hebrews 13:8 GNB). The God who created the cosmos still exists! The one who died so that sin no longer is a barrier for us is alive and unchanged! The Spirit who has promised to be our companion in this life walks with us daily! In a world full of changes, God is still the same.

And yet ... change is not easy. At the very least, it is uncomfortable. At the very worst, it can turn our world upside down! How do we live in a world full of change, knowing that a changeless God is watching over us? That's what this study is all about. It is an invitation to be honest about the surprises, interruptions, and disappointments we face on a daily basis, but it's also an invitation to consider how our relationship with Jesus guides us and comforts us in the midst of change.

And it's an opportunity to learn from one another. Surely, other members of your small group will have experienced changes similar to those which confront you right now. Their journey will enlighten you, their friendship will encourage you, and their prayers will hold you up in the uncertain days ahead. As you face the future, may you do so with utter and complete confidence ... for a change!

Opening Prayer

Lord God, we know we live in a changing world; everything about our lives is in a constant state of flux. Everything, that is, but you. We claim you as our anchor and our source of hope in turbulent times. Draw near to us now as we explore the changes we have faced in our lives, and prepare us to face the future in faith. In Jesus' name we pray. Amen.

For Starters

Take a few minutes in your group to list in the space below, as many "cultural changes" that members have seen in their lifetime. (The list might include "Sunday shopping," color television, divorced pastors, and the fall of the Iron Curtain. Is anyone old enough in your group to have lived through The Great Depression?) Have some fun with it!

Social Sexual 'orientations'   Computers / Phones
      Divorce   Internet
   Addictions

When you have assembled your list, consider which of the changes have most affected our world positively, and which have been most negative.

A Word From Others

*For everything there is a season, and a time for every
    matter under heaven:
A time to be born, and a time to die; a time to plant and
    a time to pluck up what is planted;
a time to kill, and a time to heal; a time to break down,
    and a time to build up;
a time to weep, and a time to laugh; a time to mourn,
    and a time to dance;
a time to throw away stones, and a time to gather stones
    together; a time to embrace, and a time to refrain
    from embracing;*

10

a time to seek, and a time to lose; a time to keep, and a
time to throw away;
a time to tear, and a time to sew; a time to keep silence,
and a time to speak;
a time to love, and a time to hate; a time for war, and a
time for peace.
— Ecclesiastes 3:1-8 (NRSV)

The only one who really likes change is a wet baby!
— Unknown

Don't waste your time wondering why;
Time has no answers, time passes by.
And whatever questions life arranges,
The answer is, the answer changes.
— Bob Peterson, age sixteen

In December of 1999, as the world awaited the beginning of a new millennium, *Life* magazine published its list of the 100 most important events of the second millennium (from 1000 A.D. to 1999 A.D.). The number one event was Johann Gutenberg's invention of the movable type printing press in 1450 A.D. Incidentally, number three on the list was The Reformation, and the work of Martin Luther in 1517. Imagine all the changes in the world that are directly related to these two men and their "discoveries."

Getting Personal

I remember the day they took away my typewriter! I had been using an IBM correcting Selectric typewriter for more than ten years, and I had become rather proficient on it, but some members of the church board were convinced that the church needed to enter the computer age, so each staff person was trained to use a new tool, and then dates were set to install them in our offices.

My computer was the last to be installed. I resisted, I pleaded, I even considered changing the locks on my office door, to ensure that my old "friend" would continue to produce sermons, lists, and letters. But one Tuesday morning, upon entering my office, something was tragically wrong! The "Selectric" was gone; replaced by a television set! It was, in fact, a computer terminal.

Other staff members howled in laughter when they heard that my typewriter had been absconded, but it wasn't funny to me! I was intimidated by this hi-tech box. I didn't understand how computers worked, and the thought of pushing the wrong button actually kept me awake at night. I was afraid of looking stupid.

So, there the computer sat, without even being turned on, for about four weeks. Sermons were written by hand. Letters were scrawled out and sent to the secretary to be typed. I was hanging on to the past because the future looked too scary. It seemed easier to cling to the past than to walk with uncertainty into the future.

As I now consider my life, I cannot imagine functioning without a computer! Producing sermons is so much easier. Corresponding with family and friends via email is a snap. And shopping for airline tickets, and finding a church to worship in while on vacation, and checking on sports scores from last night is done with the push of a button. What would I do, if I had never traded in that correcting Selectric?

Isn't that the dilemma with change? Even when it is positive or productive, it may still frighten us. Only when we look back at change can we see redeeming value in it, and how we have grown from the experience.

Discuss This

1. Can you think of a time that you were confronted with change in your life ... change that was required of you? Describe that circumstance ... and how you reacted to that potential change.

    Loss of 1st job. Paniced. Worked to all hours.

2. What has happened since then? Has the change been positive or negative? Were your fears or concerns realized, or was it a smooth and painless transition?

Positive for a long time
Not smooth or painless

3. What is it about change that is so bothersome?

Looking At Scripture

"Do not let your heart be troubled; believe in God, believe also in Me. In My Father's house are many dwelling places; if it were not so, I would have told you; for I go to prepare a place for you. If I go and prepare a place for you, I will come again and receive you to Myself, that where I am, there you may be also. And you know the way where I am going."

Thomas said to Him, "Lord, we do not know where You are going, how do we know the way?" Jesus said to him, "I am the way, and the truth, and the life; no one comes to the Father but through Me. If you had known Me, you would have known My Father also; from now on you know Him, and have seen Him."

— John 14:1-7 (NASB)

About The Text

1. What do you suppose the disciples were concerned about when Jesus made his announcement?

How to find Jesus. The loss of Jesus

2. How would their lives be changed by Jesus' departure?

He was their leader. They literally followed him around.

3. Do you think Jesus should have made this announcement to his disciples, or simply allowed the situation to unfold without warning?

Yes He should have made the announcement

4. Though upsetting at the time, how would the disciples ultimately perceive this "change" in their lives? Positively or negatively?

Going A Bit Deeper

The purpose of this small group is *not* to put you in an uncomfortable setting; however it might be used to stretch your comfort zone a bit. By sharing as much as you are comfortable sharing, consider the following questions in your group:

1. Have you experienced a transition recently that you can share with the group? Where are you now in this transition?

Right in the midst

2. Are you anxious about a change in the immediate future? Can you share that situation with your group?

    Yes

3. How might God use this small group in your life?

    To be there for me when it happens
    To help me stay balanced thru it.

Closing Prayer

This week, your leader will close your small group meeting in prayer. If you have a need or a prayer request, your leader will be happy to include that concern in this time of prayer.

For Further Reading

Anderson, Leith. *Dying for a Change*. Bloomington, Minnesota: Bethany House Publishing, 1998.

Frost, Gerhard. *The Color of the Night*. Minneapolis: Augsburg Publishing, 1977.

Simundson, Dan. *Hope for All Seasons*. Minneapolis: Augsburg Publishing, 1998.

Swindoll, Charles R. *Living on the Ragged Edge*. Waco, Texas: Word Publishing, 1985.

Small Group Covenant

Please read and sign this covenant as your commitment to the people in your small group. It is not intended to be a legalistic list of rules, but an agreeable process for the duration of your small group meetings.

During the duration of this study, I agree to
- Make attendance a priority
- Remain open-minded to new thoughts and ideas
- Share my thoughts, feelings, ideas, and opinions
- Respect the thoughts, feelings, ideas, and opinions of others
- Maintain the confidentiality of all that is shared
- Pray for the leader and the members in my group
- Trust that God is working through this small group experience

Signed _____ Date _____

Session Two
Dealing With The Changes Of Growing Up

"We are fearfully and wonderfully made!" So say Dr. Paul Brand and Philip Yancey in a book by that title. God ushers us into this world as screaming infants, but he surrounds us with people to love us and care for us. At birth, we are totally dependent upon our family for survival, but almost immediately, we begin the process of becoming independent. It is the very nature of childhood and adolescence.

There was a time when growing up was rather easy and uncomplicated. Everyone in the neighborhood knew us, and many pairs of eyes monitored our activities (remember the African proverb "It takes a village to raise a child"?). Most children spent all of their childhood years in the same house, and grandparents lived nearby. Many of us grew up wanting to follow in our parents' footsteps; boys wanted to pursue their fathers' occupations and girls wanted to grow up and be whatever their moms were. Our options were limited, our choices were few, and our futures were somewhat prescribed, but there was a sense of security about our lives.

Hello! It's a different world today! Children grow up faster now. They are certainly exposed to more temptations, and at a younger age, than ever before. Today's youth are generally not influenced by extended family, observant neighbors, or the guidance of school, church, and community, as they once were. Today, independence is accelerated by the fact of parents working away from home, and the unique schedules single-parent and blended families create. Finally, the availability of information through the internet has dramatically changed what adolescence is.

The purpose of this session is not to nostalgically reminisce about the good old days. Rather, it is an opportunity to recount the transitions we encountered in those formative years, and to understand how those changes shaped us. Also, this discussion is designed to grasp the transitions that today's young people endure

17

(perhaps your children or your grandchildren?), and how we might draw near to them, and help them weather the storms of these potentially tumultuous years.

Graham Nash wrote some powerful lyrics concerning parenthood in his song, "Teach Your Children." His plea to "hippie" parents was to maintain a standard, a code, for their offspring. The plea was also to the children to be more tolerant and accepting of their parents, knowing that in the end they are loved.

Opening Prayer

God, you know the joy and delight of the growing up years; every day is filled with wonder and exciting new things. But these years can also be filled with frustration, loneliness, disobedience, and doubt. As we gather to reflect on our own childhoods, remind us of the people and events that made a difference, and then fill us with the desire to make the difference in the lives of young people today. Amen.

For Starters

Take a moment and think back to junior high school. Remember the house or apartment where you lived in those years? Now, describe your favorite room in that house. What were the colors, the smells; what was the lighting like? And finally, what made it so comfortable for you?

My bedroom. Pink - canopy bed; very feminine
Chandleer that Dad made. I loved it.
My getaway.

Or ... What was your favorite time of day when you were in high school? Why?

Night time
could not wait to leave the house
felt panic if I had to stay

Or ... Who was the most influential person in your life when you were sixteen years old?

MOM !
She loved me unconditionally

Isn't it amazing how vivid the details can become when we think about the past? It is an indication of just how impressionable we are at a very young age. Some of the thumbprints are positive; some are painful to recall. But many of them have contributed to who we are today. Now, consider the young ones in your circle today; they are equally impressionable. How significant to them is a word of encouragement, or an unsolicited note, or even a gentle word of correction at the appropriate time?

A Word From Others

His life began with all the classic handicaps and disadvantages. His mother had been married three times; his father died before he was born. His mother gave him no affection, no love, no discipline, and no training in those early years. She even forbade him to call her at work. Other children would have nothing to do with him. At the age of thirteen, a school psychologist commented that the boy probably didn't know the meaning of the word "love." During adolescence, the girls would have nothing to do with him and he fought with the boys.

As a young adult, he failed academically and then dropped out of high school. He joined the Marines but the other Marines laughed at him and made fun of him. In time, he was court-martialed and thrown out of the military. When he eventually married, his wife belittled him, ridiculed his sexual impotence, and ultimately divorced him.

Finally, in silence, he pleaded no more. No one wanted him. No one had ever wanted him. He was perhaps the most rejected man of our time. Then, one day,

19

he arose, went to the garage and took down a rifle he had hidden there, and brought it to his newly-acquired job at a book storage building. And shortly after noon on November 22, 1963, he sent two shells crashing into the head of President John Fitzgerald Kennedy. That "most rejected man of our time" was, of course, Lee Harvey Oswald.

— Dr. James Dobson
*Hide or Seek: How to Build
Self-esteem in Your Child*

Children, it is your Christian duty to obey your parents always, for that is what pleases God. Parents, do not irritate your children, or they will become discouraged.
— Colossians 3:20-21 (GNB)

Getting Personal

It's a story I've told many times. When I was growing up, my father was part-owner of a family business; a century-old construction firm. Since I was my father's oldest son, he had carried with him the dream that I would one day continue the tradition handed down from his grandfather. He was certain that I would be a fourth generation contractor.

It was my senior year of high school when I told my dad of my plans to go to college. He knew that I wanted to get an education, but he thought it was merely a pre-curser to coming to work at "the plant." However, his plans were not my plans; I wanted to be a high school physical education teacher. "A teacher! A teacher? Why don't you come out to the plant to work?" "Because I want to be a physical education teacher."

Several years later, after some unplanned twists and turns in my life, I felt the call to go to seminary. Now, it was my senior year in college, and I went to my dad to tell him of my new dream. "Dad, I am going to be a minister." "A minister! A minister? Why don't you be a physical education teacher?"

My dad never told me in so many words that he was disappointed in me, but I felt it. I lived with the realization that his hopes and dreams for me were never realized. For the longest time, I felt like I had failed my dad, but late in his life, he confided in me that he was very proud of my career path. On one hand, I was overjoyed with his affirmation. But on the other hand, I wish he had told me earlier. I wanted to please him, but I went through many of my adult years feeling like the prodigal son, wasting my life in my dad's eyes.

Discuss This

1. In what ways is it more difficult to grow up today than when you were a youth? In what ways is it easier?

   Social media

   Less abuse?
   Better education

2. Did you experience any "changes" during childhood that affected your growing up? (for example, divorce, a family death, moving, a childhood illness)

   Mom's death

3. Listen carefully to the words of the Crosby, Stills, Nash, and Young song, "Teach Your Children." What do you make of the line "... And so, become yourself ..."?

   To become who God made them to be

21

Looking At Scripture

And He said, "A man had two sons. The younger of them said to his father, 'Father, give me the share of the estate that falls to me.' So he divided his wealth between them. And not many days later, the younger son gathered everything together and went on a journey into a distant country, and there he squandered his estate with loose living.

"Now when he had spent everything, a severe famine occurred in that country and he began to be impoverished. So he went and hired himself out to one of the citizens of that country, and he sent him into his fields to feed swine. And he would have gladly filled his stomach with the pods that the swine were eating, and no one was giving anything to him. But when he came to his senses, he said, 'How many of my father's hired men have more than enough bread, but I am dying here with hunger! I will get up and go to my father, and will say to him, "Father, I have sinned against heaven, and in your sight; I am no longer worthy to be called your son; make me as one of your hired men.'

"So he got up and came to his father. But while he was still a long way off, his father saw him and felt compassion for him, and ran and embraced him and kissed him. And the son said to him, "Father, I have sinned against heaven and in your sight; I am no longer worthy to be called your son." But the father said to his slaves, "Quickly bring out the best robe and put it on him, and put a ring on his hand and sandals on his feet; and bring the fattened calf, kill it, and let us eat and celebrate; for this son of mine was dead and has come to life again; he was lost and has been found.' And they began to celebrate.

"Now his older son was in the field, and when he came and approached the house, he heard music and dancing. And he summoned one of the servants and began inquiring what these things could be. And he said to him, 'Your brother has come, and your father has killed the fattened calf because he has received him back safe and sound.'

"But he became angry and was not willing to go in; and his father came out and began pleading with him. But he answered and said to his father, 'Look! For so many years I have been serving you and I have never neglected a command of yours; and yet you have never given me a young goat, so that I might celebrate with my friends; but when this son of yours came, who has devoured your wealth with prostitutes, you killed the fattened calf for him." And he said to him, 'Son, you have always been with me, and all that is mine is yours. But we had to celebrate and rejoice, for this brother of yours was dead and has begun to live, and was lost and has been found.' "

— Luke 15:11-32 (NASB)

About The Text

1. Are you the oldest child or a younger child in your family? Which is it easier to be?

   in this scenario I'm the oldest
   My brother & I are both the oldest

2. How would you describe the younger son in the parable?

   irresponsible
   impulsive

3. How would you describe the older brother?

   responsible
   obedient

4. Did the father do the right thing, giving the younger son his inheritance early and letting him go off? What do you think would have occurred if the father had refused and made his son stay home?

> Father should have known son
> & that he could not handle the
> responsibility - Father was wrong

5. What would have been the greater display of love: letting the son go, or making him stay?

> Making him stay - tough love

6. Did the older brother have a point or did the older brother have "issues"?

> Older brother had a point

7. If the story continued, or we revisited the family a year later, what do you imagine would be happening?

> Depends on if younger son
> had 'hit bottom' or if
> he was just continuing to
> use father.
> Has he turned from his old ways

Going A Bit Deeper

This is the "optional" portion of the study. You are invited to participate, but not required to do so.

1. If you could magically change one aspect of your growing up years, what would that be? How would your life be different today? *Mom do not had goten cancer, My world would be 100% different.*

2. Is there an "emerging adolescent" in your family right now? Can you share any observations you have made about the journey they are on?

   No.

3. What can the group pray for as you close?

Closing Prayer

Though some may be uncomfortable with "group prayer," it is a wonderful way to join in prayer, and build community at the same time. The leader will open with a brief prayer and anyone who wishes may add one sentence to his/her prayer.

For Further Reading

Dobson, James. *Hide or Seek*. Old Tappan, New Jersey: Fleming H. Revel, 1974.

Thielicke, Helmut. *The Waiting Game*. New York: Harper And Row, 1959.

Session Three
Dealing With The Changes Of Growing Older

Henri Nouwen writes in *Sabbatical Journey: The Diary of His Final Year*:

> The big event tonight was the soccer match between Germany and the Czech Republic, which my father and I watched on television. I will always remember the Czech goalkeeper. He played an astonishing game; many times he prevented the Germans from scoring. His agility, courage, foresight and iron nerves made him, in my eyes, the great hero. But in overtime, when the match was 1-1, he couldn't hold on to the ball that the German player shot into his hands, so he was the reason why the Germans, not the Czechs, received the European Cup from Queen Elizabeth. He will be remembered, not as a hero, but as the man who failed to give the Czech Republic its victory. While the Germans were dancing on the field, embracing one another, crying with joy, and raising their arms victoriously, this talented goalkeeper sat against one of the goalposts, his head buried in his knees. Nobody was there for him. He was the loser.
>
> I felt deeply moved by the image of the defeated goalkeeper. All his great performances will be forgotten, in light of one mistake that cost the Czechs the greatly desired European Cup. I often wonder about this "final mistake." After a long and fruitful life, one unhappy event, one mistake, one sin, one failure can be enough to create a lasting memory of defeat. For what will we be remembered? For our many acts of kindness, generosity, courage and love, or for the one mistake we made toward the end?

To grow old is to grow afraid. In the latter years of our lives, we are filled with worries and concerns about so many things; health, finances, our dependence upon others, our spouse, our children, our grandchildren. We may be afraid of dying, afraid of death itself, and, as Henri Nouwen described above, afraid of what will happen to our legacy after we die. All of this comes in the time of our lives when we should be enjoying leisure time after a lifetime of labor. Does it have to be this way?

This study is about growing older; about being honest about our fears, but also sharing in the joys of being older, wiser, perhaps having more free time than we have had since our childhood. It will be a time to explore what it means to grow older in a culture that seems to value youth. Finally, it will be a time to plot the future! It will be a time to explore what tasks and experiences God has yet in store for our lives. Even in these golden years, we can have a say in what we say, do, feel, act, and become! I trust that this study will bring you hope and joy!

Opening Prayer

God of grace, your promise is to be our companion in this journey of life. When we rejoice, you rejoice. When we are afraid, you comfort us. And when we lose our way, you call us back home. Help us to look to our future in faith, and trust that you will be with us all along the way. Amen.

For Starters

1. What is the earliest memory of your childhood? What has changed about the world since then? (For example, as I write this, I am remembering a time when I was about three years old, standing on a stool, doing dishes with my grandmother who lived with us. What has changed? For starters, grandparents don't live with their grandchildren much anymore. Few people do dishes by hand now; we have machines for that! And rarely would a child count doing dishes as a pleasant memory! Now it's your turn.) *Bear from aunt Nell*

   Cooking Mac + Cheese   Mimmie's house + dresses
   Lunch at park across street   Riding on tractor + dolly
   Sand box + swing set in back yard Buick Painting go cart
   Playing w/ baby dolls Camping Learning to ride bikes

2. What is the message that our culture sends regarding aging? (for example, in the media, commercials, in health clubs, and even in the church)

   Less valuable as you age

3. What is the "down side" of growing old? What's the "up side"?

   Poor Health   *Time*
   Dependance

29

A Word From Others

"And you know what? The strangest thing."
"What's that?"

"I began to enjoy my dependency. Now I enjoy when they turn me over on my side and rub cream on my behind so I don't get sores. Or when they wipe my brow, or they massage my legs. I revel in it. I close my eyes and soak it up. And it seems very familiar to me.

"It's like going back to being a child again. Someone to bathe you. Someone to lift you. Someone to wipe you. We all know how to be a child. It's inside of all of us. For me, it's just remembering how to enjoy it.

"The truth is, when our mothers held us, rocked us, stroked our heads — none of us ever got enough of that. We all yearn in some way to return to those days when we were completely taken care of — unconditional love, unconditional attention. Most of us didn't get enough. I know, I didn't."

... "Mitch, it is impossible for the old not to envy the young. But the issue is to accept who you are and revel in that. This is your time to be in your thirties. I had my time to be in my thirties, and now is my time to be seventy-eight."

— Mitch Albom
Tuesday's with Morrie, 1997

Youth; too bad it's wasted on the young.

— Mark Twain

Eighty isn't old ... if you're a tree!

— Anonymous

Be still my soul; your God will undertake
To guide the future as he has the past
Your hope, your confidence let nothing shake
All now mysterious shall be bright at last.

— Katherina von Schlegel, b. 1697
"Be Still My Soul"

Getting Personal
My Legacy

Step One

At what age do you think you will die? (This may be derived from family history, your health, or simply your hunch. Make your best guess.) Put that number here: _____80_____

Step Two

What would you like to have your loved ones say about you upon your death? (Imagine them standing around your grave, reminiscing about your life; what would you want them to say?) Write your answer here:

Kind loving gracious

Step Three

How old are you now? Subtract this number from "Step One" above and write the difference here: _30_____

This is how long you have to shape your legacy. Very seldom does one want their legacy to say "He had a huge investment portfolio" or "She always had a clean oven" or "He worked sixty hours per week all his life." And yet, the way we live our lives, and the priorities we have displayed will one day be our legacy.

I first learned this exercise in the D.Min. program at Bethel Theological Seminary in Arden Hills, Minnesota, taught by Dr. Frank Green.

Looking At Scripture

*And when the days for their purification according to
the law of Moses were completed, they brought Him up
to Jerusalem to present Him to the Lord.*

*And there was a man in Jerusalem whose name was
Simeon; and this man was righteous and devout, looking for the consolation of Israel; and the Holy Spirit
was upon him. And it had been revealed to him by the
Holy Spirit that he would not see death before he had
seen the Lord's Christ. And he came in the Spirit into
the temple; and when the parents brought in the child
Jesus, to carry out for Him the custom of the Law, then
he took Him into his arms, and blessed God, and said,
"Now Lord, You are releasing Your bond-servant to
depart in peace, according to Your word; for my eyes
have seen Your salvation, which you have prepared in
the presence of all peoples, A LIGHT OF REVELA-
TION TO THE GENTILES, and the glory of Your people
Israel." And His father and mother were amazed at the
things which were being said about Him.*

Anna means grace

*And there was a prophetess, Anna the daughter of
Phanuel, of the tribe of Asher. She was advanced in
years and had lived with her husband seven years after
her marriage, and then as a widow to the age of eighty-
four. She never left the temple, serving night and day
with fastings and prayers. At that very moment she came
up and began giving thanks to God, and continued to
speak of Him to all those who were looking for the re-
demption of Jerusalem.*

— Luke 2:22, 25-33, 36-38 (NASB)

About The Text

1. What adjectives can you use to describe Simeon? And Anna?

Righteous devout

32

2. Who are the "Simeons" and "Annas" in our world today?

Nuns, pastors,

3. Have there been people like Simeon and Anna in your life; older persons of faith who have nurtured you or blessed you? What contribution have they made?

Not religiously

4. How could the church provide opportunities for older saints and younger saints to connect?

This Bible study

Going A Bit Deeper

1. What thing(s) would you like to yet accomplish in your life?

More service   less paycheck
More community

2. What one thing would you like to see occur in this world before you die?

More toward Christianity instead of away
Grandchildren
Nathan's faith to increase
Flying cars

3. What are you most fearful of at this stage in your life?

Illness

Closing Prayer

At this session, share one thing in your life for which you would welcome prayer. Your Small Group Leader will assemble a list, and pray for each. Then, next session, he/she will ask how that "issue" is progressing. Please trust your leader, and your fellow members, as you share this request for prayer (but know that "passing" is always an option). Amen.

For Further Reading

✝ Carter, Jimmy. *Living Faith*. Westminster, Maryland, Times Books, 1998.

Kimble, Melvin and McFadden, Susan, editors. *Aging, Spirituuality and Religion: Volume II*. Minneapolis: Fortress Press, 2003.

Nouwen, Henri J. M. *Sabbatical Journey*. Bethany, New York: Crossroad Publishing, 1998.

transition from working in the world to working for God.

Session Four
Change Happens
When Families Grow

Imagine the different ways that families can increase in size:

- A young couple gives birth to their first child ... or second ... or fifth!
- There is a wedding, and a daughter-in-law or son-in-law is now "family."
- A blended family provides grandma and grandpa with four new grandchildren.
- Flight 797 brings a new baby brother all the way from India.
- After six years of grief, a widower moves on with his life, and finds a new love.
- New Member Sunday at church brings in 23 new brothers and sisters.

In many of these scenarios, there is great joy and delight! New family members are celebrated and welcomed with warmth and love. Sometimes, new family members bring hardship, competition, conflict, or confusion. Growth can be messy! In other words, when families grow, it can be a good thing *and* a bad thing. But this much is known for sure: "Change happens when families grow."

This session focuses on the changes that occur when we add people to our families. In previous sessions, I have provided stories to illustrate these changes, but in this session, I will ask you to provide the stories. How has your "family" grown over the years? Who came in, how did your family change, and were the changes positive or negative? If we define the family broadly enough to include our "church family," what feelings do you have about your new brothers and sisters in our congregation? (Not every aspect of this study will apply to every member of your group. Part of the time you will find yourself sharing, and at other times, listening.)

As a pastor, I can honestly say that growing families are among the most joyful events in ministry! Celebrating the birth of a new child, officiating at the marriage of a son or a daughter, or witnessing an adoption is such a privilege and a wonderful occasion. However, I must also say that these events — in every instance — these events make life more complicated than it was before. True for parents. True for siblings. True for grandparents. True for churches. It's universal!

According to one influential marriage and family institute, the top three causes of conflict in marriage are: money, sex, and in-laws. However, if the couple is a "blended family" (a family comprised of children from a previous relationship) the fact of being a "blended family" promises to be one of the top three sources of marital conflict.

So, why do we choose to complicate our lives in this way? It is because God creates us to be in relationships. They can be messy and confusing and even painful at times, but relationships are what make life meaningful and full. In our next session, we will face the issue of grief and loss head-on, so enjoy this rather lighthearted look at the family as it grows!

Opening Prayer

Lord, you have created us to be connected with one another, through families, friendships, congregations, and communities. Thank you for the new people you have sent into our lives. In these moments of small group study, may we be honest about the changes we have experienced, and how these changes have shaped our lives. In Jesus' name. Amen.

For Starters

1. When is the last time your family experienced a new-comer? Share that experience with the group.

   Susan

2. Have you ever been "the new-comer"? How did that feel? How were you received?

   Yes. Let in but not all the way.

3. Would you describe yourself as a "new-comer" or an "old-timer" in your church? How does your status ("new" or "old") affect how you feel about the growth at your church?

   New comer

A Word From Others

If there's one thing that she didn't need, it was another hungry mouth to feed, in the ghetto.

— Elvis Presley
"In The Ghetto"

For this reason a man shall leave his father and his mother, and be joined to his wife; and they shall become one flesh. — Genesis 2:24 (NASB)

In an agrarian society, children are an asset; sons help their fathers farm, daughters help their mothers cook *and clean. In a suburban family, children are a liability! It costs $85,000 to raise a child from infancy to high school graduation today. What do you get for your investment? A Christmas card!*

— Anthony Campolo, Sociologist

Getting Personal

As you consider church life in the first century, is there anything that remotely resembles your congregation in the twenty-first century? For example, in your congregation:

- Are miracles and wonders every displayed?
- Are all your members in close fellowship?
- Do people share their belongings/finances with one another?
- Do you gather in homes to share meals with glad hearts?
- Are your fellow members in "good will" with each other?
- And is the Lord adding to your number?

Is there any reason why the characteristics of the first-century church shouldn't be present in twenty-first century churches? Why do some churches fail to display some or all of these qualities?

Discuss This

1. Talk about how your life changed when you had children.

   "I remember two distinct changes in my life when our son was born. I was in youth ministry — an expert, some people said. When I became a parent, I saw children from a different perspective; I wasn't the expert anymore, suddenly they scared me to death! The other change was that I became much less self-centered. My time, my money, my "stuff" slid way down the list of importance, and my child moved to the top."

38

A. In what ways did your life change when your children came along?

Love grew!

B. What "surprised" you about parenthood?

Easy + fun

C. What is the most difficult thing about raising children?

Getting him to sleep

2. Talk about how your life changed when a marriage happened.

"Pam and Tom had three sons, Adam, Justin, and Alex, and their lives were largely spent in basketball gyms, wrestling rooms, and baseball fields! This year, Pam's Christmas card arrived at our house, with a picture of their family at Justin's wedding; included in the picture was Jennifer. Pam wrote five words on the card that said it all: "I finally got my daughter!"

Any stories of courtship, weddings, or transitions involved with welcoming a new member into the family?

A. How do you treat the son-in-law or daughter-in-law differently than you treat your own child?

B. Has the marriage of your son or daughter brought you closer
    to them, or do you feel more distant?

3. Talk about grandchildren — How have they changed your life?
        "I don't know, maybe it's because I was so busy when my
    kids were small, and now that I'm a grandfather, I have more
    time, but I notice so much more of what they do! I watch my
    grandchildren more intently than I did my own children, I see
    the little things, and I don't ever remember noticing my kids
    do those things."

    A. How do you respond to the above description by this grand-
        father? True for you?

    B. Have you had any conflict with your children about the
        way they parent?

    C. There is an increasing number of grandparents raising
        grandchildren today. What are the pluses and minuses of
        this sort of relationship?

40

4. Talk about our "church family" and how growth has affected it.

   "I joined First Lutheran because it was a small church. Now that it is growing, I'm not sure I like that very much."

   "Well, I joined First Lutheran because it's a growing church, and if it were small and unchanging, I'm not sure I'd like that very much."

   A. Do you think God wants all churches to grow? Why or why not?

   B. What are the most positive changes in a church that has grown?

   C. What are the negative aspects?

5. Talk about adoption, step-children, second marriages, and empty nests.

   "I was invited to watch a child be delivered. Sounds odd, I know. But this child was two years old, and he arrived on a plane from Calcutta, India. Never have I seen such love and joy. Never have I seen older siblings so lovingly welcome a new brother into their family. Except for the fact that he was black and his new family, white, one would never guess that he hadn't been biologically born into their family. Oh, and the child's name? "Jeevan." In India, it means "Life." Yes!

A. What are the unique challenges of raising an adopted child?

B. Have you had any experience welcoming in a new "parent" because your birth mom or dad died, or because your parents divorce? Can you share your experience?

Yes

C. Family experts expect that blended families will have conflict. What is your response to this? Is it inevitable? What are the issues of raising children in blended families?

D. When our children become independent and "move out" (at least for a while!), what adjustments do we make?

Total A. Felt rejected.

Looking At Scripture

Many miracles and wonders were being done through the apostles, and everyone was filled with awe. All the believers continued together in close fellowship and shared their belongings with one another. They would sell their property and possessions, and distribute the money among all, according to what each one needed.

Day after day they met as a group in the Temple, and they had their meals together in their homes, eating with glad and humble hearts, praising God, and enjoying the good will of all the people. And every day the Lord added to their group those who were being saved.
— Acts 2:43-47 (GNB)

About The Text

1. Do you think this fellowship was without a conflict?

No

2. This group was growing daily. New saved members were becoming part of this community. What problems would this cause?

3. What strengths could come from adding new members?

Going A Bit Deeper

Before you close this session, take a few moments to share within your group what changes you are experiencing in your life right now. Since our first session, some members may have had an illness or death in their family; others may have experienced unemployment, a new job, a new home, or some other significant life-event. It will offer the group a chance to consider prayer concerns or the need for practical help (such as meals, encouragement, or job networking).

You might also consider a "social event" for your small group at this half-way point. How about attending a movie together? There are several movies that would spark some great after-movie-dinner-conversation on this theme of "change." (For example, *Cheaper by the Dozen* [PG], *Something's Gotta Give* [PG13], or your could rent *About Schmidt* [R], which has to do with retirement and loss.) Enjoy!

Closing Prayer

Gracious God, as these most important aspects of our lives grow and change, may our ability to love, adapt, grow, and change along with them. Teach us, Lord, to be open and loving to the new people who come into our lives. Amen.

Session Five
Change Happens When
Families Decrease In Size

Three stories of grief:

Kyle and Melissa were married on a hot, humid August Saturday at Minnetonka Lutheran Church, and I had the privilege of officiating at their wedding. Everybody that they loved, and that I loved, was there, and our celebration was wonderful! It was also the last time I saw my dad. On Monday evening, I received the call that my dad had died of a heart attack, apparently in his sleep. For many weeks, it felt as if someone had kicked me in the stomach. As a pastor, I had lots of experience dealing with families and death. As a son, grief was new, and excruciating, and relentless.

• • •

On a cold February day, I jumped into the cab of a U-Haul truck, while Marsha and our two small children followed in the Buick. All of us were weeping. We had lived in this house for five years, enjoyed wonderful neighbors, a loving church, and deep, lasting friendships. Now we were moving to a new community 1,500 miles away, but our hearts were firmly planted in the old. Again, our grief was real, and it lasted for many, many weeks.

• • •

The phone call came late one afternoon: our best friends had separated and filed for divorce. "Gerald" was my best friend in adulthood, "Ginny" was a soul mate to Marsha, and the four of us, and our children, were like family. Vacations, projects, late-night pizza, holidays; we shared it all, and now it had all been undone. The proverbial "who is the least likely couple to separate?" That was Gerald and Ginny. We were so sad ... for them ... for us. And we realized that it changed our relationship with each of them forever.

45

These are my grief stories, but you have your own. Just recalling them brings back many of the feelings and much of the pain. Someone once defined grief as "the pain of letting go." I think that's right. Eventually, the pain subsides, but it is never really totally erased. Such is the imprint that grief leaves upon us.

Last session was lighthearted, perhaps trite, as we considered the change that happens when our "family" grows larger. Birth, marriage, new neighbors, and friends; it's all joy! But this session is very much the opposite, as we consider the change that is associated with grief and departure. Please be sensitive to one another in this session; share your thoughts and feelings, and even the growth that has come as a result, and know that God is present in your group as you describe the painful change that has come to your lives.

Opening Prayer

God of comfort, you know the grief of letting go. Your own Son died so that we might live, and you watched him go to the cross. Be with us now as we speak of pain and loss, and reveal your healing and tenderness to each of your children. Amen.

For Starters

1. Can you share your earliest memory of a death? It might be a grandparent, or a neighbor; perhaps it was even a pet? What do you remember about that experience? How did it impact you (change you) as a child?

grand uncle → grandfather

Very indignant / angry
needed, to help
needed someone to be mad at

2. On perhaps a lighter note, did anyone "move out" of your house when you were growing up? (A sibling going off to college, or an older sister or brother getting married?) What were the emotions of that experience? Were you glad because there was more

46

space for you, or were you lonely because you missed the one who left?

A Word From Others

I am a better rabbi because of Aaron's death. I am a more empathetic counselor, a wiser pastor, and a more sensitive friend. But I would trade it all away in an instant to have my son back!
— Rabbi Harold Kushner,
When Bad Things Happen to Good People

"To cleave" means "to stick to like glue." When a couple is married, it is like two pieces of paper being glued back to back. When they divorce, it is impossible to do so without damaging both pieces of paper.
— Author unknown

If God were good, He would wish to make His creatures perfectly happy, and if God were almighty, He would be able to do what He wished. But the creatures are not happy. Therefore, God lacks either goodness, or power, or both. This is the problem with pain.
— C. S. Lewis

Grief is a natural part of human experience. We face minor grief almost daily in some situation or another. To say a person is deeply religious and therefore does not have to face grief situations is ridiculous. Not only is it totally unrealistic, but it is also incompatible with the whole Christian message.
— Granger Westberg,
Good Grief

47

Suffering often brings out the worst in people. When the going gets rough, most of us do not become patient saints. More likely, suffering leads to self-centeredness, crankiness, and anger toward God and other human beings. Sufferers are not very lovable. It's hard to hang in there with a sufferer.

— Dan Simundson,
Where is God in My Suffering?

Anything that doesn't kill makes me stronger.
— An Olympic gymnast

Getting Personal

Three more stories of grief. Many years ago, Marsha led a Bible study with a group of high school girls. They were bubbly, curious, fun-loving, energized, moody, bright, and expressive. In short, they were typical teenage girls. But in a matter of a few short months, three of their lives would dramatically change.

One of these joyous teenagers lost her pastor/dad through a heart attack. He survived the first episode, rallied for a month as prayers were prayed and answered, and then one night he died, and her world suddenly crashed. The second teen was also a pastor's daughter. She noticed the conflict between her parents escalate that spring, and by midsummer, dad moved out ... and in ... with a younger woman. Another life crashed. The third teen also experienced a tragedy, and her life also changed dramatically. Her dad, a fixture in the community, was accused of sexually molesting a young boy. There was community uproar at this *obviously* false accusation. Friendships were tested, rumors rumbled throughout the community, and ultimately, evidence mounted that substantiated the young boy's accusations. The teenage girl watched as her family became unraveled. Three young girls, three totally different circumstances, but the common thread among them was loss and grief.

1. It would be unfair to suggest that any of these girls had an easier time than another, given their context. That being said, do you think any of these girls had a societal "prescribed" way of acting and grieving their situation? (In other words, is there a "normal" way to navigate each of these situations?)

No

2. How would you have answered each of these girls if they had asked, "Where was God when this was happening in my life?"

There beside you (footprints)

Looking At Scripture

Now a certain man was sick, Lazarus of Bethany, the village of Mary and her sister Martha. It was the Mary who anointed the Lord with ointment, and wiped His feet with her hair, whose brother Lazarus was sick. So the sisters sent word to Him, saying, "Lord, behold, he whom You love is sick." But when Jesus heard this, He said, "The sickness is not to end in death, but for the glory of God, so that the Son of God may be glorified by it." Now Jesus loved Martha and her sister and Lazarus. So when He heard that he was sick, He then stayed two days longer in the place where he was.

Then after this He said to the disciples, "Let us go to Judea again." The disciples said to Him, "Rabbi, the Jews were just now seeking to stone You, and are You going there again?" Jesus answered, "Are there not twelve hours in the day? If anyone walks in the day, he does not stumble, because he sees the light of this world. But if anyone walks in the night, he stumbles, because the light is not in him." This He said, and after that He said to them, "Our friend Lazarus has fallen asleep; but I go, so that I may awaken him out of sleep." The disciples then said to Him, "Lord, if he has fallen asleep, he will recover." Now Jesus had spoken of his death, but they thought that He was speaking of literal sleep. So Jesus then said to them plainly, "Lazarus is dead, and I am glad for your sakes that I was not there, so that you may believe; but let us go to him." Therefore Thomas, who is called Didymus, said to his fellow disciples, "Let us also go, so that we may die with Him."

So when Jesus came, He found that he had already been in the tomb four days. Now Bethany was near Jerusalem, about two miles off; and many of the Jews had come to Martha and Mary, to console them concerning their brother. Martha therefore, when she heard that Jesus was coming, went to meet Him, but Mary stayed at the house. Martha then said to Jesus, "Lord, if You had been here, my brother would not have died. Even now I know that whatever You ask of God, God will give You." Jesus said to her, "Your brother will rise again." Martha said to Him, "I know that he will rise again in the resurrection on the last day." Jesus said to her, "I am the resurrection and the life; he who believes in Me will live even if he dies, and everyone who lives and believes in Me will never die. Do you believe this?" She said to Him, "Yes, Lord; I have believed that You are the Christ, the Son of God, even He who comes into the world."

When she had said this, she went away and called Mary her sister, saying secretly, "The Teacher is here and is calling for you." And when she heard it, she got up quickly and was coming to Him. Now Jesus had not yet come into the village, but was still in the place where Martha met Him. Then the Jews who were with her in the house, and consoling her, when they saw that Mary got up quickly and went out, they followed her, supposing that she was going to the tomb to weep there. Therefore, when Mary came where Jesus was, she saw Him, and fell at His feet, saying to Him, "Lord, if You had been here, my brother would not have died." When Jesus therefore saw her weeping, He was deeply moved in spirit and was troubled, and said, "Where have you

laid him?" They said to Him, "Lord, come and see."
Jesus wept. So the Jews were saying, "See how He loved
him!" But some of them said, "Could not this man, who
opened the eyes of the blind man, have kept this man
also from dying?"

So Jesus, again being deeply moved within, came
to the tomb. Now it was a cave, and a stone was lying
against it. Jesus said, "Remove the stone." Martha, the
sister of the deceased, said to Him, "Lord, by this time
there will be a stench, for he has been dead four days."
Jesus said to her, "Did I not say to you that if you be-
lieve, you will see the glory of God?" So they removed
the stone. Then Jesus raised His eyes and said, "Fa-
ther, I thank You that You have heard Me. I know that
You always hear Me; but because of the people stand-
ing around I said it, so that they may believe that You
sent Me." When He had said these things, He cried out
with a loud voice, "Lazarus, come forth." The man who
had died came forth, bound hand and foot with wrap-
pings, and his face was wrapped around with a cloth.
Jesus said to them, "Unbind him, and let him go."

— John 11:1-44 (NASB)

About The Text

It's only two miles from Jerusalem to Bethany, and when Jesus heard the news of his good friend Lazarus, he probably could have been there in a matter of hours. However, by the time Jesus arrived, Lazarus had been dead for four days. (Jewish tradition suggested that after three days, a person was "really dead.") These facts are important in understanding and discussing this story.

1. What were the emotions of Mary and Martha toward Jesus?

where have you ben
felt abandoned

51

2. In spite of their emotions, what evidence of their faith is present in the story?

Martha
They understood his power
Martha knew he was God
Mary understood his power

3. Is it okay to vent anger at God?

yes
Jews were sarcastic in saying (see how Jesus loved him")

4. How would Mary and Martha's lives change in view of Lazarus' death?

Their faith was confirmed
They started church
were at his death

5. John 11:35 is the shortest verse in the entire Bible. What does it teach us about Jesus?

Jesus wept

6. Is there anything in this story of grief that resembles any "grief story" in your life?

Why did Jesus cry?

Going A Bit Deeper

This is the fifth lesson; the fifth time you have been together as a small group. I am going to ask you to stretch out of your comfort zones in these next few minutes.

Obviously, it is always acceptable to "pass." But I encourage you to participate as fully as you are able.

1. Can you share one of your grief stories? It might relate to a death, a divorce, a job loss, a disability, a move, or any other transition in your life that has caused pain.

2. How did your life change in light of your grief experience? Can you relate it to Rabbi Kushner's quote from *When Bad Things Happen to Good People*?

3. Are you in the midst of a grief experience right now? Perhaps it is too fresh to share, but if you dare, your small group members will partner with you on your journey.

4. How are grief and suffering affected by the following resources? (See the story of Job.)

   A. Prayer

   B. Scripture

   C. Worship

   D. Friends

   E. Meditation

Closing Prayer

God of mercy, in our pain and sadness, when we are most alone, we turn to you. You listen to your children as we pray, you draw near to us and hold us up when there is no hope. Be with each person in this room, reveal yourself to us as we journey through the difficult chapters of our lives, and remind us of your power and grace. Amen.

For Further Reading

Albom, Mitch. *Tuesdays with Morrie*. New York: Doubleday, 1997.

Bell, Steve and Valerie. *Real Survivors*. Ann Arbor, Michigan: Vine Books, 2003.

Frost, Gerhard E. *The Color of the Night*. Minneapolis: Augsburg Publishing, 1983.

Kushner, Harold. *When Bad Things Happen to Good People*. Westminster, Maryland: Random House, 1981.

Lewis, C. S. *The Problem of Pain*. New York: MacMillan Publishing, 1962.

Simundson, Daniel. *Where is God in My Suffering?* Minneapolis: Augsburg Publishing, 1983.

Westberg, Granger E. *Good Grief*. Minneapolis: Fortress Press, 1962.

Changing Cities, Changing Jobs, Changing Churches

The joke goes something like this; After a shipwreck, a man was stranded on a deserted island for 22 years. When a rescue boat finally came, they noticed three buildings on the island. "What are those buildings?" they asked. "Well," said the man, pointing to the buildings, "that's where I live, and that's where I go to church ... and that's where I used to go to church!"

Changing churches; people do it often. But we also change houses, change cities, change jobs, change cars, and change cell phones with regularity. Often, in fact, most of the time, we do this by choice. This study will focus on the transitions of our lives that are choices rather than a consolation prize. I hope you will freely offer your own perspectives of the changes in your lives that have brought you into different places in your lives. Enjoy!

Opening Prayer

Lord, if life is a journey, we each travel incredible paths. Where we go, our destinations, are important; where we settle down and what we become. But the journey is important as well. Teach us to take joy in the journey, knowing that wherever we go, you go with us. In Jesus' name. Amen.

For Starters

Each member of the group, on a piece of paper, take a moment to inventory your life. Make a list of:

- Your favorite house
- Your favorite car
- Your favorite job
- Your favorite vacation place

As you share your list around the group, let each person describe *one* of these, and tell your group why you liked it and why you changed it. In other words, why did you choose to move from that house ... or why you left that job? Are there reasons for changing even the good, positive things in our lives?

A Word From Others

Our souls are not hungry for fame, comfort, wealth, or power. Our souls are hungry for meaning, for the sense that we have figured out how to live so that our lives matter....

— Rabbi Harold Kushner

We must realize that risk is at the very core of the Christian life. You're not called to be safe from all of life's troubles, simply secure in the knowledge that you are "roped to" the living Christ.

— Tim Hansel
You Gotta Keep Dancin'

When I was young, I always prayed to God that I would be somebody. Now, I wish I had been more specific!

— Lily Tomlin

Do not worry then, saying, "What will we eat?" or "What will we drink?" or "What will we wear for clothing?" For the Gentiles eagerly seek all these things; for your heavenly Father knows that you need all these things.

— Matthew 6:31-32 (NASB)

Getting Personal

If I didn't say this anywhere else in this study, it would need to be said here, or it would be a major omission! Marsha (that would

58

be my wife!) has probably endured more change in her life because of my decisions than anyone should ever have to! Never mind 28 cars in 32 years of marriage. Never mind sixteen different living situations (apartments, town homes, even a pop-up tent one summer!). The fact that, because of job changes, I have taken her to nine different communities in these years is beyond the call of duty.

But, let me describe to you Marsha's response every time we have moved: refusal, reluctance, resignation, relocation, and rejoicing. It's a little bit like the stages of grief when we move, and with every move, the pattern has been nearly the same. I am so grateful to her, because while Marsha hates change, she does it with astonishing grace.

Do you identify with these stages of "change grief"? Can you speak of a time when you moved, or changed jobs, or changed churches, and went through this sort of pattern? Even if you were the one who made the choice for change, are the stages still present? Spend a few minutes discussing this.

Looking At Scripture

Some time later Naomi heard that the LORD had blessed his people by giving them good crops; so she got ready to leave Moab with her daughters-in-law. They started out together to go back to Judah, but on the way she said to them, "Go back home and stay with your mothers. May the Lord be as good to you as you have been to me and to those who have died. And may the LORD make it possible for each of you to marry again and have a home." So Naomi kissed them good bye. But they started crying and said to her, "No! We will go with you to your people."

"You must go back, my daughters," Naomi answered. "Why do you want to come with me? Do you think I could have sons again for you to marry? Go back home, for I am too old to get married again. Even if I thought there was still hope, and so got married tonight and had sons, would you wait until they had grown up?

*Would this keep you from marrying someone else? No,
my daughters, you know that's impossible. The LORD
has turned against me, and I feel very sorry for you."*

*Again they started crying. Then Orpha kissed her
mother-in-law good bye and went back home, but Ruth
held on to her. So Naomi said to her "Ruth, your sister-
in-law has gone back to her people and to her god. Go
back home with her."*

*But Ruth answered, "Don't ask me to leave you!
Let me go with you. Wherever you go, I will go; wherever you live, I will live. Your people will be my people,
and your God will be my God. Wherever you die, I will
die, and that is where I will be buried. May the LORD's
worst punishment come upon me if I let anything but
death separate me from you!"*

*When Naomi saw that Ruth was determined to go
with her, she said nothing more.*

— Ruth 1:6-18 (GNB)

About The Text

The story of Naomi and Ruth is a story of change. Naomi's husband dies, and after her two sons marry, those two sons also die. Naomi wants to send her two daughters-in-law back to their mothers, back to their own hometowns. Orpha goes, but Ruth cannot do so. She chooses to stay with Naomi. "Your people shall be my people, your God shall be my God; and wherever you go I shall go."

1. What would you have done if you were Ruth? Stayed with Naomi, a person who was not your blood relative, or gone back to your own hometown? Why?

2. When is it right to "follow blindly" a person who is taking you through change; when is it appropriate to drag your feet and try to change their plan?

3. If you are unhappy at a church, when is the right time to leave?

4. How do you know when change is inspired by God, or if it is a symptom of restlessness, or fear, or failure, or ambition?

Going A Bit Deeper

1. What is your greatest fear of change in the next six months?

2. What one thing have you learned about yourself because of change?

Closing Prayer

Lord, we come to you in faith, because we don't know what the future holds. When sudden changes touch our lives, draw us close and remind us that wherever we go, you are already there! Amen.

For Further Reading

Hinkle, Mary E. *Signs of Belonging*. Minneapolis: Augsburg Publishing, 2003.

Kushner, Harold. *When All You've Ever Wanted Isn't Enough*. New York: Simon & Schuster, 1986.

Session Seven
As The World Turns:
Changes In Our Culture

Every generation has its transitions. In the 1960's, an era of challenging authority was ushered in, as government leaders, educators, law enforcement, clergy, and parents found themselves no longer able to command attention and respect. Now it had to be earned. In the '80s it was the beginning of the "information age." In just one generation, we went from knowing nothing about computers, to relying upon computers for nearly every task in our lives. Y2K (remember that scare?) could not have happened in 1960, but as a result of the progress of the 1980s technology gurus, the fear of a new millennium became very real in 2000.

However, I would suggest that the transition to a new millennium did not actually begin on January 1, 2000; rather, it began on September 12, 2001. On that day, America awoke to the startling realization that we were not invincible. And to be more accurate, the real transition did not happen as a result of the terrorists attacks on September 11, 2001. Change had been percolating for many years. The point is, it's a different world than it was just four years ago. The fear of another terrorist attack is real, and it has affected politics, the economy, air travel, the church, major league baseball games, and the sale of duct tape!

But fear over other changes in our society also abounds. Many are concerned that "outsourcing" will move their jobs overseas. Others fear for their children's safety in the halls at school, or on the playground, or even at a church outing. People today are nervous about the economy, nervous about a war, nervous about anthrax, and whoever heard of "road rage" or AIDS or no-fault divorce a generation ago? Truly, it's a different world than the one many of us grew up in, and certainly the one our parents grew up in. What can we do with all these uncertainties and fears that swirl around us and those we love? That's a question just waiting for an answer!

This session, perhaps more than any other, is a reprise of Merv Thompson's claim that "the only two certainties in this life are Jesus Christ and change." But one truth does remain; that those who believe in Jesus Christ can know peace in the midst of chaos because the kingdom of Jesus will reign forever, and we will be a part of it. May this session give you hope, not based on national security, or financial prosperity, or simplistic piety, but rather, on the unchanging majesty of God.

Opening Prayer

Gracious God, we confess that we are often afraid. When enemies attack us, or when we feel alone, or when our faith seems like a mustard seed compared to the complicated issues of life, our fear can be overwhelming. Remind us that you are with us in every circumstance. Amen.

For Starters

1. Think of a time in junior high school when you were afraid. What was it that caused the fear? A certain teacher? A school bully? A family problem? Fear of punishment from your parents? Looking back, was that fear justified? Why or why not?

2. What would be "the list" of the things kids are afraid of today? Are those fears justified?

3. There is such a thing as "healthy fear." When is fear a good thing?

4. What changes has the church undergone in your lifetime that excite you? What changes disappoint or offend you?

A Word From Others

A Christian congregation is not a sanctuary from the world, but a window on what God, in Christ, is doing in the world.

— Pastor Mary E. Hinkle

Fear not that your life shall come to an end, but rather that it shall never have a beginning.

— John Henry Newman

Come gather 'round people, wherever you roam
And admit that the waters around you have grown
And accept it that soon you'll be drenched to the bone
If your time to you is worth savin'
Then you better start swimmin' or you'll sink like a stone
For the times, they are a-changin'

— Bob Dylan

The 1990s have turned out to be a tough time for pastors. The North American church is traveling through a transition period in history. No one knows where we are going. Nevertheless, church members expect their pastors to know.

— Pastor Leith Anderson,
A Church for the 21st Century

God's Word for ever shall abide, no thanks to those who fear it
For God himself fights by our side with weapons of the Spirit
Were they to take our house, goods, honor, child or spouse,
Though life be wrenched away, they cannot win the day
The Kingdom's ours forever!

— Martin Luther,
"A Mighty Fortress Is Our God"

Sometimes he calms the storm; other times, he calms his child.

— Lyrics by Tony Wood and Kevin Stokes,
"Sometimes He Calms The Storm"
Recorded by Scott Krippayne

Getting Personal

In the spring and summer of 2004, I was given a fifteen-week sabbatical by my congregation. What a gift! I read, I relaxed, I played golf and fished, and I spent nine weeks in Europe "breathing Luther." I lived in Wittenburg for several weeks, and then traveled to the cities and sites that molded Luther's life into a bold and radical agent for church change. It was a time I will never forget!

However, while I was gone, some amazing things back home changed. Because there was very little English media available to me, I was oblivious to the fact that President Ronald Reagan died, that Iraq had become a sovereign nation, or that Tampa Bay had won the Stanley Cup. At home, my wife rearranged the furniture, the grass seed I spread just before I left had become lush and green, and our favorite next-door neighbors divorced, sold their house, and moved. At church, two staff people resigned their positions, five new families joined our congregation, and the property committee planted 35 shrubs and nine mature evergreen trees! All of this happened while I was away, so when I returned, there was a bit of culture shock for me. Had I been here, I would have absorbed the changes as they unfolded; however, since I was gone when these changes occurred, I had the feeling that my world was coming apart at the seams.

Change is always happening; gradually, but we don't seem to notice change when it is a part of our everyday lives. Think of it this way: When we are with our small children every day, we may not notice their growth. But when Grandma and Grandpa visit, after not seeing their grandchild for three weeks, the child's growth is monumental.

Some changes in this world go unnoticed because we have chosen to ignore them. If we are disgusted by the news, we might stop reading the newspaper. If we resent the changes at church, we may stop attending for a while. It is when we remove ourselves from the changing culture that change overwhelms us. "Cocooning" does not prevent change from happening; it merely delays our awareness of it. Therefore, the more aware we are of our culture — of the world in which we live — the more adaptable we will be to the inevitable changes that occur.

1. In what ways have you seen people (perhaps even yourself) cocoon, and therefore, become isolated from change in the world?

2. What are ways that people in your community can help guide and effect change? What are the ways (if any) that they can inhibit change?

Looking At Scripture

God is our shelter and strength, always ready to help in times of trouble. So we will not be afraid, even if the earth is shaken and the mountains fall into the ocean depths; even if the seas roar and rage, and the hills are shaken by the violence. There is a river that brings joy to the city of God, to the sacred house of the Most High. God is in that city, and it will never be destroyed; at early dawn he will come to its aid. Nations are terrified, kingdoms are shaken; God thunders, and the earth dissolves. The LORD Almighty is with us; the God of Jacob is our refuge. Come and see what the LORD has done. See what amazing things he has done on earth. He stops wars all over the world; he breaks bows, destroys spears, and sets shields on fire. "Stop fighting" he says, "and know that I am God, supreme among the nations, supreme over the world." The LORD Almighty is with us; the God of Jacob is our refuge.

— Psalm 46 (GNB)

This is called "Luther's Psalm" probably because it was this text that provided the inspiration for his most noted hymn, "A Mighty Fortress Is Our God." There is something comforting about this psalm that draws us in and causes us to feel a sense of peace. Perhaps it is the repeated phrase, "The Lord Almighty is with us; the God of Jacob is our refuge." Or perhaps it is in the listing of God's omnipotent ability to end wars, to still our hearts, to calm the seas, and to make sense out of the chaos of our lives. Or maybe it is simply in knowing that, even 400 years before Christ, people were afraid of tumultuous change, and sought God's protection and grace, just like us!

68

On September 12, 2001, at a prayer service following those horrific terrorist attacks, Psalm 46 provided the verses we focused on. Our world was shaken by violence! Our people were terrified! We needed to cling to a promise that there was a God who is ultimately in control of this planet! A sanctuary filled with anxious adults and children heard the soothing voice of God whisper, "Be still and know that I am God, supreme among the nations, supreme over the world."

About The Text

1. In considering Psalm 46, how has God been a "refuge and shelter" for you? Be as specific as you can be.

2. Have you ever seen God's hand intervene in disaster, distress, or chaos in the world?

3. Discuss the following words (images) and how they might relate to the church and Christian life:

   A. "A river that brings joy...."

B. "A city where God dwells...."

C. "The thunder of God...."

D. "Being still...."

4. There are many promises in this psalm, however not all of them have come to be. What do you make of the psalmist's promise that "... He stops wars all over the world; he breaks bows, destroys spears, and sets shields on fire"? Why hasn't God delivered on these promises?

5. How does this psalm speak to the changes — both the minor changes and the enormous changes — that are unfolding in our world?

Going A Bit Deeper

1. Is there an issue pending in your life right now that, if God were to intervene, it would alter the course of your life? Have you prayed about that? Can you share it with your small group so that they can pray about it?

2. It's been said that we often task God to change circumstances, but that God sometimes changes us. Has that ever been true for you?

Before you gather for your final small group discussion, take a few moments to dream! While no one but God knows the future, try to imagine what your life will be like ten years from now. Have some fun with it, but try to project where you'll be living (or *if* you'll be living!), your job, your children, your hobbies. Jot these down below and come prepared to share next time.

Closing Prayer

Gracious God, we know that the world in which we live is constantly changing, and confess that we are sometimes afraid. Turn our fear into hope, give us wisdom to effect positive change in our setting, and allow us to embrace the changes that make this world a more loving, caring place. Amen.

For Further Reading

Anderson, Leith. *A Church for the 21st Century*. Minneapolis: Bethany House Publishers, 1992.

Hansel, Tim. *Holy Sweat*. Dallas: Word Publishing, 1987.

Sweet, Leonard. *Carpe Manana*. Grand Rapids, Michigan: Zondervan Publishing, 2001.

Session Eight
The Future!

"Jesus Christ is the same; yesterday, today, and forever." With those words of the Apostle Paul, we have come full circle. In light of all the changes in our culture, our world, our homes, churches, schools, and families, we cling to that one constant: that God is changeless.

Throughout the course of this study, you have experienced changes, too. Some have had children come or go, others have had job transfers, terminations, or promotions. Maybe you moved into a new home, or bought a new car, or have had an intimate relationship that has come undone. If so, this study has been a sort of "laboratory" for you. Others in your small group have nurtured you through; the studies, hopefully, have provided you with provocative questions to ponder, and of course, you have learned firsthand — again! — that God is only a prayer away. In the midst of the change, you have been surrounded by God's Spirit, God's Word, and God's people.

But what about the future? In this span of months, so much change has happened, so what sort of changes does the future hold? Your small group will likely disband, your focus on "change" will end with this study, but still you will be deeply affected by changes in your life. And in the dark nights of the soul, you will perhaps be afraid of the changes that are to come. My prayer is that you will flashback to this final session, as you ponder the changes that are yet to come, because in this session there is hope! I wish you all the best!

Opening Prayer

God of creation, you know the future and the past; you know our lives intimately. As we consider the future, may we do so with confidence, knowing that wherever we go, and whatever we do, you will be our comfort and our guide. Bless us and keep us, in Jesus' name. Amen.

For Starters

At the end of session seven, you were given a homework assignment: to jot a description of what your life will be like ten years from now. It is total speculation, but your list is likely to be a wonderful mix of goals, dreams, fears, faith, humor, and imagination. Share your descriptions around the group, and have some fun with it!

A Word From Others

Yesterday is gone, tomorrow is not yet here, but today is a gift; that's why it's called "the present"!

— Anonymous

The best way to look at the future is with your back toward it!

— Pastor Philip Natwick

Any fool can count the seeds inside an apple; only God can count the apples in one seed.

— Dr. Robert Scheuller

Some people think being a Christian is akin to this; you are stalled in a brutal Minnesota blizzard, and then God arrives in some heavenly tow truck, delivers hot cocoa to you in the cab, and then hauls you to safety. The truth of the matter for Christians is this: We are trapped in a blizzard, and God comes and sits with us in the cab of the truck until the storm passes. That's what it means to be a Christian.

— Robert Farrar Capon

If you come to a fork in the road, take it.

— Yogi Berra

Don't worry about anything, but in all your prayers ask God for what you need, always asking him with a thankful heart. And God's peace, which is far beyond human understanding, will keep your hearts and minds safe in union with Christ Jesus.
— The Apostle Paul in Philippians 4:6-7 (GNB)

Getting Personal

Nobody knows the future. Agreed? We might be able to look ahead a day or two and assume what's going to happen, but beyond that, we don't have a clue as to what the future holds. In some ways, that's too bad. If I knew IBM stock was going to soar in value next month, I'd sell my house, take the proceeds, and buy all the "big blue" I could! If I knew for certain that the Twins would win the World Series in October, I'd find a way to get to Las Vegas and put a month's salary on them, but since I do not know these things for sure, it is too great a risk to assume that they will come to pass.

On the other hand, sometimes not knowing the future is best for us. If you knew that you were going to die in eighteen months, your life would likely be miserable. If you knew that your son would grow up to be an addict or a convicted felon, you might choose not to have children. What if you knew you would go into work one day next month and be fired? Knowing the future would negatively affect the present.

You see, life is both a risk and an adventure. There is a certain risk in getting out of bed in the morning, but we usually are willing to take that risk with no guarantees of the future. By the same token, taking that risk is what makes life exciting and fun. Knowing what is around every bend would be boring! Knowing what was going to happen every moment of our lives would become monotonous and dull. Would we really want to know the future?

But Someone does know the future ... every moment of it ... because he created the concept of time. God, in his wisdom, knows what will happen every moment of your life. He knows the joy that is to come, and he knows the sorrow. (Why he doesn't prevent the bad stuff from happening is one of life's greatest mysteries, but we are convinced that he knows it all.) Trusting a God who knows the future ... in fact, holds the future ... is probably one of the greatest sources of comfort to Christian people. God is omni-everything! (They're called "the Omnis": God is omniscient because he is all knowing, omnipotent because he is all powerful, and omnipresent because he is everywhere.) Perhaps the greatest evidence of the omni's Psalm 139.

Looking At Scripture

LORD, You have examined me and you know me. You know everything I do; from far away you understand all my thoughts. You see me, whether I am working or resting; you know all my actions. Even before I speak, you already know what I will say. You are all around me on every side; you protect me with your power. Your knowledge of me is too deep; it is beyond my under-standing.

Where could I go to escape from you? Where could I get away from your presence? If I went up to heaven, you would be there; if I lay down in the world of the dead, you would be there. If I flew away beyond the east or lived in the farthest place in the west, you would be there to lead me, you would be there to help me. I could ask the darkness to hide me or the light around me to turn into night, but even darkness is not dark for you, and the night is as bright as the day. Darkness and light are the same to you.

You created every part of me; you put me together in my mother's womb. I praise you because you are to be feared; all you do is strange and wonderful. I know it with all my heart. When my bones were being formed, carefully put together in my mother's womb, when I was growing there in secret, you knew that I was there — you saw me before I was born. The days allotted to me had all been recorded in your book, before any of them ever began. O God, how difficult I find your

*thoughts; how many of them there are! If I counted them,
they would be more than the grains of sand. When I
awake, I am still with you.*

*O God, how I wish you would kill the wicked! How
I wish violent men would leave me alone! They say
wicked things about you; they speak evil things against
your name. O LORD, how I hate those who hate you!
How I despise those who rebel against you! I hate them
with a total hatred; I regard them as my enemies.*

*Examine me, O God, and know my mind; test me,
and discover my thoughts. Find out if there is any evil
in me and guide me in the everlasting way.*

— Psalm 139 (GNB)

About The Text

How much do you know about David, the psalmist who penned
these words? Perhaps you know that he was Israel's greatest king;
from shepherd boy to ruler of God's people in a few short years!
He killed Goliath in a single shot. He was a faithful and obedient
follower of God, and Jesus came from the lineage of David. But
did you know that David was also an adulterer, a murderer, and a
liar? He initiated an affair with a woman named Bathsheba. Then
he had her husband, Uriah, sent to the front lines in battle, where
David knew that Uriah would be killed, and then he lied to cover it
up. What a man of contradictions!

But the point David makes in Psalm 139 is that God knew all
this about him, and still God guided, and blessed, and journeyed
with David over a lifetime. The future ... that "thing" that is always
just around the corner ... was as unpredictable for David as it is for
us. Had he known what was to come — both the good and the bad
— he would have shuddered to move forward. But God knew, and
he filled David with enough courage to live it out.

Going A Bit Deeper

There are three tremendous truths in this psalm which are worthy of our consideration and discussion. Please take the time to do that now.

Truth Number One

There are no secrets from God! He knows everything that we think, say, and do.

1. If God already knows everything we think, say, and do, why do we need to pray? Why do we need to tell God our sins (confession)? And why do we need to ask God for specific things, if he already knows?

2. Have you ever tried to hide something from your parents? Can you share any of that?

3. This truth illustrates God's unconditional love. Are humans capable of this sort of love for one another?

Truth Number Two

We are never (ever!) out of God's mind.

1. Do you ever feel far away from God? Why is that?

2. Are you — in fact — far away from God when you have these feelings?

Truth Number Three

God knows how and when our lives will end ("every day of my life was written in your book before any of them had ever begun").

1. Does this seem like "predestination"? Does that violate your sense of free will?

2. What is the greatest fear you have about the end of your life? (For example, is it in the act of dying, the potential suffering, the concern you have for those you leave behind, or does it have to do with the afterlife?)

3. Why is it significant that our days are recorded in God's "book"? Set aside the concerns you may have had regarding predestination and consider instead, God's interest and love for you. (Do you keep baby books for your children?)

A Closing Thought

Remember "Black Monday"? The stock market dropped that day by 508 points; it was a greater percentage drop than the market slump in 1929 that sent the nation into The Great Depression.

I was serving a congregation in Oregon on Monday, October 19, 1987. On Tuesday, October 20, I received a call from Jim and Heidi (names have been changed to protect their identity), asking me to come to their home that evening. Jim owned a small company that was extremely profitable, and it allowed him and his family to have everything; a beautiful home with acreage and horses, a boat, a mountain home, country club membership. The works! But Jim told me that he was severely marginalized in the market. That means that he was buying stock on credit, with his business as collateral. When the market crashed, the loans came due. Immediately.

That next day, Jim was losing his business, his mountain home, his two cars, and all that he had set aside for his children's education. All gone. Heidi and Jim were in anguish. They were finished. Their livelihood, their reputation in the community, their security, their dreams would all be lost by the next day. Their future was black.

Seven years later, as I prepared to leave Oregon for another congregation, Jim took me aside and reminded me of that terrible night. He said it was the lowest point of his life. He also said it was the turning point in his life! His faith, and Heidi's faith, too, had soared in the seven years since Black Monday. His commitment to his family was renewed, their appreciation for their friends deepened, their love for their church was increased, and their trust in

God became the anchor of their lives. All of this happened as a result of this single, tumultuous day.

You see, Jim and Heidi thought the future was secure, but they learned what all of us eventually learn; that life changes. They learned that the future is uncertain, always uncertain. Ironically, the worst thing ever to happen to them became the best thing that ever could have occurred. Because now their future is secure. It's not a cliché, it is truth. For Jim and Heidi, for Marsha and me, and for you, friend, the only certainties in this life are Jesus Christ and change.

Thanks be to God!

Closing Prayer
(Pray this benediction out loud together)
As you go on your way, may Christ go with you
May he go before you to show you the way
May he go behind you to encourage you;
Beside you to befriend you, above you to watch over
Within you to give you peace. Amen.

For Further Reading
Barna, George and Hatch, Mark. *Boiling Point.* The Barna Group <www.barna.org>.

Kushner, Harold. *When All You've Ever Wanted Isn't Enough.* New York: Simon & Schuster, 1986.

CPSIA information can be obtained
at www.ICGtesting.com
Printed in the USA
FSHW011103230119
55205FS